Finding Her

Sherri, I hope you enjoy Finding Her!
Kristie

poems by

Kristie L. Williams

Finishing Line Press
Georgetown, Kentucky

Finding Her

Copyright © 2022 by Kristie L. Williams
ISBN 978-1-64662-936-7 First Edition
All rights reserved under International and Pan-American Copyright Conventions.
No part of this book may be reproduced in any manner whatsoever without written permission from the publisher, except in the case of brief quotations embodied in critical articles and reviews.

ACKNOWLEDGMENTS

Main Street Rag—Arid Harvest At High Tide
Dan River Review—Dance With The Duende, Lost In Transmission, Requiem
Maximum Tilt Solstice Anthology—A Diggers Lot
Madness Muse Press— Womanhood, Responding To Words Written on the Slate of Her Vagina
Hermit Feathers Review—Embracing Gilead, In Another Life Molly Woods, Insomnia
Heron Clan 8—Crying Over Spilled Milk
Nostos: Journal of Poetry, Fiction, and Art—Watching You Undress Me

Publisher: Leah Huete de Maines
Editor: Christen Kincaid
Cover Art: Megan Merchant
Author Photo: Lorien C. Stocks
Cover Design: Elizabeth Maines McCleavy

Order online: www.finishinglinepress.com
also available on amazon.com

Author inquiries and mail orders:
Finishing Line Press
PO Box 1626
Georgetown, Kentucky 40324
USA

Table of Contents

One Minute 1
How to Drown in a Dry Shower Stall 2
Lost in Transmission 3
Morning 5
Glitzed at the Gym 6
Yoga Pants 7
Crying Over Spilled Milk 9
Dance with the Duende 10
Requiem 12
In Another Life Molly Woods 13
Responding to Words Written on the Slate of Her Vagina 14
A Refracted Moment 15
Gilded Cage 16
Portrait of a Magpie 17
For The Maladjusted Gardener Who Would Be Culled By
    Her Own Brown Thumb 18
Arid Harvest at High Tide 19
Hands Clean 20
Embracing Gilead 21
Womanhood 22
Insomnia 24
The Funeral 25
Vanishing Point 26
The Body Sings Autonomous 27
Watching You Undress Me 28
I Went To a Wedding on Your Birthday 30
A Digger's Lot 31

For Marty Silverthorne
I hope you're reading over my shoulder

One Minute

To Be Who I Was;
To Grieve My Loss;
To Take Stock of What I Have;
To Accept it All;
To Strategize a Forward Move;
To Imagine One Foot in Front of the Other;

Before Quietly Stepping Into
Who I Am Now.

How to Drown in a Dry Shower Stall

You warn…

the hot water will leave its red
finger marks up and down my body;

when the water begins to limp
lonely with cold,

its icy scorch will burn purpled welts
deep into milky untouched skin.

caught in the confusion of your
 hysteria,

my silent screams
choke;

my vocal cords
spasm;

not even my tongue is wet
when my cracked lips tinge blue with realization

your fear is something I'll never be able to lay
my willowy fingers on…

in your presence.

Lost In Transmission

The day I Left My Childhood Home
for Parts
Unknown
Was My First
Lone Adventure

I Decided to Take the Scenic Route

I Stopped When I Came Upon
What Seemed-to-Be
an Endless Patch of
Green

In the Middle of this
Wide Open Space
My Bare Feet
Settled
into the
Soft Grass

My Toes Danced
as a Breeze Ruffled the
Textured Blades
Back and Forth

My Hands Sank
Deep
into the
Rich Dark Earth

Cool and Wet

I Could Have Sworn
I Felt Its
Pulse

Seedlings
Planted and Nurtured
Could Most Certainly
Serve Plenty

Any Dream Could have Thrived Here

I Sat in the Stillness
Plotting My Course

I Stood
Ever-So-Gently
Leaving My Imprint

Walking Back to My Car
Inner Spirits Trusted Themselves

Now
I No Longer Take the Scenic Route on Visits Home

Randomly Dumped Chemicals
Do Not Discriminate

LiFe-Giving Strands
Mirror
Choking Weeds

Careless Steps
have Crushed
Supple Blooms

Time is Marked by Those Who
Track Seasons in an
Antiquated Almanac

Time and Space are
Barren Now

Morning

Water cool & clean
splashes brightly on my face
rolls long down my neck

Glitzed at the Gym

Walking away from my workout,
i'm paused mid corridor—

As a budding ballerina pirouettes
her exit from dance class;

She sports a black leotard, white stocking feet,
and bejeweled tennis shoes;

Her chauffeur is wearing landscaping gloves and a ball cap
—sunglasses resting on the bill—

The pastel pink Hello Kitty knapsack slung over his right shoulder
compliments a plain black tee stretched across his chiseled frame;

In his left hand, a hot pink Barbie lunch tote
answers the glitter teetering on the tip of his nose—

Yoga Pants

Shopping at Targét;
I see them and smile

...Remembering wearing a similar pair
(sister yogas)

These are heathered grey;
a teal roll-down band
provides a backdrop for
slivered leopard spots

...Remembering my legs
strong & shapely—

Used to plant my feet,
raise my bottom,
bridge all my strength,

My sister yogas
assisted that derriere move—

Squeezing tight
lifting body parts into
perfect poses—

...My abs never carved;
But, always flat stood at attention
saluting the colored swath
that kissed my belly button &
nuzzled its bejeweled ring—

I have to try these on;
snatching them off the rack
I glide into the fitting room

Just outside my stall door
a full length mirror waits

...My eyes alight with hope
as they adjust to the reflection—

A fellow shopper smiles
behind me
"*Oh you precious thing*
those yoga pants hug your love bundle"

...And just like that
my belly button's unintentional smile

Opened wide the veil
swaddling my all too unrealistic fantasy—

Lost somewhere between
not pregnant and not even almost flat.

Crying Over Spilled Milk

Flagged down in the parking lot…

A friend's Aunt T,
(twice-removed)

Presents her with nipple guards ensconced by
sunshine yellow tissue paper in a lilac gift bag;

—Grocery carts stand in stunned silence—

Aunt T does not know that conception failed to keep;
or, that her mother's grand proclamation
omitted a step…

Once cloistered behind bedroom walls
tears deluge the cleft in her chin;

Dark circles of soured milk pool the front of
her heathered-grey tee;

Two hapless plastic guards lay unwrapped on the bed
as her nipples weep;

Wishing she could have simply said…

—*Thank You*—

Dance with the Duende

I

Stomp, Stamp, Tap.

Strings pull
Language Flows Like Water,
Music Listens
 to the
 Fall.

Stomp, Stamp, Tap.

Voices of Time Past
Speak
to the
Beat.

Floor Breathes
Like An Infant,

Small and Quick.

Language Flows Like Water,
Over the Banks of My Mind.

II

Oh Thunderous Heartbeat
Innocent Ears are Christened
as
Notes Bleed
with the
Ink
of this
Pen.

III

Nursery Rhymes,
Take Me Back,

Before Him,

Before It ...

The Knowledge
of All
that is
Mortal ...

Love.

duen·de
/doŏendā, ˈdwendā/

a quality of passion and inspiration.
.
(in the folklore of Spain, Portugal, Latin America, and the Philippines) a supernatural being or spirit resembling a pixie or imp.

Requiem

"Still Haven't Found What I'm Looking For"
On the Radio
Resonates with the Thought of
You
and
Another
I can still Fight to Save

Like the Moth
To a Flame
He Still Flocks

Fingers Singed
are Not
Enough

Why Walk Through Fire
Just To Feel
Numb

You
Stretched Out in Slumber
Underneath a Pink Funeral Glow
as Pictures present a
DiFFerenT
Hue

Would Your Song Give Him Pause

""Still Haven't Found What I'm Looking For" Artist: U2
Album: *The Joshua Tree* Released: 1987

In Another Life Molly Woods

You are heralded as forager of a frontier
we clamor to share—

Your words are art
devoured;

Extant nourishment for like minds seeking
satiated souls…

Love is yours
you are one with us—

But today's reality
is not a tolerant space…

Occupied by varied frequencies
accommodating alternating states of consciousness.

Such an expanded view depletes resources
allocated for persons who tout familiar currencies;

If only you were waving goodbye in a tickertape parade
tokens bestowed upon you could be kept in perpetuity…

Instead we disavow your accomplishments
contemplating your extinction.

Extant:: still existing : not destroyed or lost

Molly Woods is a fictional character from the science fiction drama series *Extant*, played by Halle Berry. The title "In Another Life Molly Woods" is a good-bye spoken to Molly from J.D. a fictional character played by Jeffery Dean Morgan.

Responding To Words Written on the Slate of Her Vagina

Wrapping your legs around the most malevolent
offerings to fall from masculine mouths;

Swallowing whole their gospels
because your own are stifled;

As long as you shrink
toward silence;

There is no context for discovering
the soul of your hallelujah.

A Refracted Moment

I watch my mother cry
desperate to reshape the asymmetrical daisy
swimming in her box of tears

Gilded Cage
(A Poem of Senryū'd Dimensions)

Pretty Wants Fill Space
False Light Blurs Cleared Door, Illumes
Knobs That Will Not Turn—

Portrait of a Magpie

A pale face smeared with the last vestiges of ill worn cosmetics
Hair matted to one side by oil and lack of lather
Clothes with designer labels hang ragged under the weight of an unseen
Ball and chain…

She is not misfortuned; contrarily, she has soured
Soaking in wine and seasoned with antidepressants—

Picking her skin until blood bursts red
Licking lacerations and quenching cracked lips
With a tumble of tears…

Always falling
On cue;

Sucking out long buried barbs
Waiting for the freedom to roll
Along the outer edge of her tongue;

Until they are spat in no
Particular direction—

Who will catch her shrapnel?

Who among us is set to cradle the pain in our arms
Grafting a new vein; or, opting to thrust it upon
Another unsuspecting soul…

Unlucky and left to watch as she garnishes her sheer sleeve
With curdled joy from the self inflicted gash—

Sculpting new scars and sowing
Seeds born of chaos;

She is an indiscriminate collector of pain.

For The Maladjusted Gardener Who Would Be Culled By Her Own Brown Thumb

Sitting at the start of a sandy path
Flanked by lush greenery,

I hear your fingers digging, as I listen to you
Pray, to a God you've said you don't believe in,

For a sinkhole, deep enough to stop
A heart at its core,

My screams reverberate
Wet with marrow,

I Am StiLL
HeRe

As ripe red roses
Bloom out of my chest,

Climb skyward arms and anchor
Themselves to extended legs,

My being is now a pergola
Built to bare the brunt of you,

I watch the earth open up and swallow you
Whole.

Arid Harvest at High Tide

Curls of Smoke Dance
Above a Glass of
Chardonnay

Cool Breeze Ruffles
Strands of Honeyed-Wheat
Falling upon my Shoulders

Crashing Waves
A Siren's Song

Still

Peace Lurks
Just Beyond My Finger Tips

Why Delve
Answers Swept
Beneath

A Surface of Perpetual Change

Hands Clean

The grime of slung dirt smears
clingy under white lather

A sickly floral scent anchors the stench of crusted venom
mingling with steam from a furious faucet

Hands held up to a bathroom mirror
pray and give thanks for artificial light

Embracing Gilead
—for Beth

Grocery store routines whirl;
produce sprayed in timed intervals
maximizes purchase appeal.

Broccoli glistens,
silver droplets breathe new life
into every stem and floret.

Mama slowly rounds the island of vegetables,
refreshed stalks bask in the mist;
her hands grasp a broccoli bouquet.

Purposefully swinging the bushy cluster to-and-fro
Mama showers her towheaded boy with silvered joy.

His bright cerulean eyes dance;
laughter envelops his body.

Two souls,
incandescent in their own right
share a blessing…

Forevermore.

Womanhood

Daddy says I used to be perfect ...
'Til I turned twelve,
Got my period,

BECAME A WOMAN.

Now I run with the wolves, he says.
Digging up the bones of others,
Piecing together a body,

A PAST.

A past of women
Whose lives place them in
Concentration camps of

CONFORMITY.

The unlucky,
The unique,
Experiment with themselves,

BELL JARS BECOME HOMES.

As the pressure builds,
Glass breaks,
The poking and prodding
Of that eternal lover
Evokes such excitement,
Voices erupt,

STICKY SWEET.

I pause,
Realizing I have not gone in search of woman,
Asking for the Ideal specimen,
I have not fought my conformity,

NOR HAVE I EMBRACED IT.

To those of you who bitch and moan ...
Do you even know why?
I sit silent,
A voice within me,

LISTENS.

I don't need to prove a past
Filled with ideals of false realities and
Experiment with contaminated souls,
I am *me*
That is enough.

Insomnia

When Chaos

                  Rattles

                                    Every
                                        Crevice

and

           Cranny

                  of the

                  Mind's Eye;

Like

                                    Scattered

        Runes…

The Funeral

He is Gone
having told me Good-bye
twenty-eight days Before
We arrived at this spot

I sit watching others
Marvel at the Box
His Life
Now rests in

It seems Absurd

the Chicken Salad
I stashed
Behind the Cake
Between the Fried Chicken
and Glass-Bottled Cokes
Resonates

People ask if I saw Him today
Still
Oblivious to the Fact

He is Not
Here

Almost blind to the tears
Streaking my face
I wipe my Nose
and Extend the Hand

Someone Violently Pulls
Away

I Smile
Remembering His Last
I Love You

Vanishing Point

She did not return to her first home;
but resides—

womb adjacent...

A place where heartbeat
echoes life abated—

And self
is a pre-drawn creation.

The Body Sings Autonomous

A vessel splayed
for seeds sown

Bleeds when gutted by
repetitive reckless reaping.

Over time,

Bones extend,
muscles stretch;

Sinews splice—

Organs shift,
beyond anticipated boundaries…

Accommodating the absence.

A bruised heart and scarred lungs
rise in awe of first solitary breaths

Her soul is her own again.

Watching You Undress Me
    (A Love Letter to Body Image)

You position me in front of the full length mirror
mounted on the back of a hushed door.

Kneeling in front of me, you unzip my left
black butter soft leather bootie and make quick work of my
sheer nylon trouser sock.

When you notice my downward gaze
boring a hole into beige carpet, you stop,
crook a finger under my chin, delicately imploring me to see my
pleasure, a glint in your eye forces me to feel the ridge of
your thumb glide heel-to-toe, both feet are exalted before
I have steadied my reflection or
chanced an exhale.

I hear my skin whisper and bare witness to desire as your
forefinger traces a keyhole cutout, the plum eyelet blouse
seems to darken as my skin pinks, and your index finger has
loosed a single sateen button, inviting you to explore the
nape of my neck, my arms raise themselves without a word,
from behind my chair, your hands move up my ribcage and
over my head, relieving the tasteful top of its modest duty.

Moving in front of me again, careful not to obstruct my view, you
search out the hidden zipper of my lilac corduroy pants, the zipper's
undoing spurs our moments, pushing up on my forearms, I lift
my bottom, you tug at my waistband, soon my thighs gleam
under soft light and string tied panties, triangled lace is the only
thing between you, my reflection, and secrets from my
nether world.

Underpinnings with crisscrossed hook-and-eye straps are floored
by the sound snap of your deft touch and the sight of twin orbs.

Not realizing my arms have x'd out my body, you tap my elbows, arms reply with a slip to the side, I see spiciness truly reflected, imperfect beauty is comfortable in its own skin—

I Went to a Wedding on Your Birthday

Drank Blue Moon
still tasted Isenbeck

Felt the effects from eight bottles of wine
a split among friends ages ago

White lights strung in a barn
brought me back to a dance floor
blurred as I spun between two points

My dance with Lorca's Duende happened
more than two years before we met

When you said hello
I knew it was you
who breathed true meaning into words I'd already written

You who had already known me for a hundred years
said it was the only love poem ever felt in your soul

I thought you would resent your question as it begged my answer
gone now
I realize
you resent that it didn't

On our last day
you borrowed my copy of Lorca's philosophy
I asked for your copy of Salinger's Nine Stories
both raw both beautiful

A tribute

Tonight I ate wedding cake
and blew out a candle

A Diggers Lot

Sitting alone
at time's end—

Recoiled by a single notion…

Only the hole she herself crafted
cannot be reconciled—

Kristie L. Williams started her writing journey to impress boys and found her true voice as a poet during her time at Saint Andrews Presbyterian College in Laurinberg NC where she earned a B.A. in English/Creative Writing. It was in that space and time that the seeds for this collection were planted.

Kristie went on to East Carolina University and received an MAEd. in Adult Education. She continued to share her love of words while teaching in the North Carolina Community College System.

After 12 years of teaching Kristie began using her own story of quadriplegia and cerebral palsy to advocate for herself and others with disabilities. She describes her work as disability adjacent, because although it shapes the context of her work cerebral palsy does not overshadow the arc of her story.

She has been previously published by *Main Street Rag, Dan River Review, Cairn, Maximum Tilt Solstice Anthology, Madness Muse Press, Hermit Feathers Review, Heron Clan 8,* and *Nostos: Journal of Poetry, Fiction, and Art.*

When she's not playing with words, she is participating in adaptive recreation, creating mixed media art, reading great books, and going to rock concerts.

CPSIA information can be obtained
at www.ICGtesting.com
Printed in the USA
JSHW060536260822
29687JS00003B/239